MY BROTHER'S KEEPER

Poems of the Vietnam war by Marine

Cpl. Rod Padilla

To Post 474

RODWICK PADILLA

Hope everyone enjoy reading this book.

"Aloha"

Rod Padilla

"pineapple"

America Star Books
Frederick, Maryland

First printing

America Star Books has allowed this work to remain exactly as the author intended, verbatim, without editorial input.

Softcover 9781634487016
PUBLISHED BY AMERICA STAR BOOKS, LLLP
www.americastarbooks.com
Frederick, Maryland

DEDICATION

To my late brother Ronald Matthew Padilla, who paid the ultimate sacrifice and to all service men and women who serve and protect our country.

"When he shall die,
Take him and cut him out in little stars,
And he will make the face of heaven so fine
That all the world will be in love with night
And pay no worship to the garish sun."
—William Shakespeare

ACKNOWLEDGEMENTS

GIVING THANKS

First and foremost, I would like to thank my wife Bernie of 37 years, without her support I would not be the man I am today. Her continuous support and encouragement kept me walking a straight line all these years. To my children Jack and Christina, grandchildren, Brandon, Ronald, Kiara and Sevena, thank you for keeping me young and on my toes. My friend and co-worker Barbara who allowed me to give speeches to students about my Vietnam experience which later sparked my passion for writing. With all of your combined love and support you made it possible for me to have the courage to revisit my past and to appreciate the present and look forward to my future.

POEMS OF THE VIETNAM WAR

INTRODUCTION

"I will return."

Those 3 words will forever ring in my head. My older brother had said this to me before he had left for Vietnam. Six months later he returned, in a green zip up bag. It was at his funeral that I decided to avenge his death. I was only 19 when I volunteered to go to Vietnam and survived a 13 month tour of duty for my brother and my country. Put your boots on and make sure they are laced up tight because you are about to go on a journey. From boot camp to Vietnam and re-introduction to society, you will experience a unique angle of struggle, courage and faith.

Uncle Sam's Finest

When your young and feeling bored
You want to do something you could not ignore
Like joining the service and being a man
Making your Dad proud of you for joining Uncle Sam

Days on end through thick and thin
You and 90 others are making a stand
Through Boot Camp it will be "Hell"
But not to worry you will fulfill

Hoping you could be the very best
Guys like you will get depressed
Because through the struggle and pain
You will have a lot to gain

Times on end, you'll fall on your face
Than there's your Sergeant picking up your pace
Humping with full packs on your back
Wondering if you will make it through the rugged tracks

Climbing, Crawling, and reaching for the Stars
Your buddies next to you breathing really hard
Sweat falling down your face
Wishing you were out of this place

"Now" we're in a dark and empty room
Wondering what surprises, is next in doomed
Wearing this mask that looks so weird
"Serge" telling us that we have nothing to fear

Seeing white smoke in front of you
Now we're all wondering what to do
Now everyone will have to remove their mask
To see if you would survive the tear gas class

Men, crying and puking all over the place
Here is your Serge yelling in your face
And now we're frantic with despair
Wanting to breathed much of fresh air

All of a sudden there was a very bright light
Which a door had opened, what a joyful sight
All 90 men, had stormed out of that room
Knowing that they all had survived the gassy perfume

Now today will be one of the hardest
When they all have to swim their farthest
With full packs on your back, and a rifle in your hand
Most likely you will hit bottom, and you will have to do it again

And now the rifle range we go
To see our Serge put on his show
He can really shoot that weapon
And make those bulls eyes in succession

You will have a week too sight in your weapon
In three positions, Sitting, Standing, and Kneeling
Now the final day is here
To not get a Medal which everyone fears

Your Graduation day is coming soon
That you will be in your final groom
You will march down the parade field
And do your very best for the final drill

Feeling proud that you've made it through
All three months of which we knew was hard to do
Putting your dress blues on
And now it time for you to move on

Now, you will find out where you'll be stationed at
Hoping you don't catch the over-seas jet
Now my Friends and I are on our way
Too South Viet Nam, we will have to stay

Thirteen months don't seem so long
Moving from place to place we often frown
Don't know where our area will be
To help those people, who want to be free

Fighting goes on day after day
Watching your friends be put away
In green Zip up bags, they all lie in a row
Lying still, as everyone will see them go

In to the plane, and back to the States
They all be sent to their land of grace
Their Families will cry from time on end
Knowing that they will never see them again

Soon it's my turn to leave this Country
Coming home not feeling so funky
Not knowing how we will be treated
Too say that our Country was defeated

I know for myself it wasn't true
If only they would let us go on and do
Take and take and move right on
And don't stop until the war was done

Counting the days on one hand
Making you feel good saying, "Let's Do It Again"
My friends had said that my stare was a little hazy
But yet they all knew I was going a little crazy

Now, I'm told to leave the country
Whom, it has been in wars through many centuries
How much longer will the war have to "go on"?
Only "God knows" it only just begun

Did my Friends, and my Brother die in vein
For not knowing, what was there we had to gain
Yes, 58,000 fellow men had died
And yet we still mourn, and still wondering why

I'm here "Today", to say my piece
To let my mind be at ease
Also to remember what we all had gone through,
I would do it again, if my country had asked me too

Cpl, Rodwick J. Padilla
USMC
Viet Nam, Veteran 66-67

The Rifle Drills You Have To Learn

Before you graduate from Boot Camp
You will learn all the Rifle Drills
Right and Left shoulder arms
Present arms, Port arms, and Attention

Parade Rest, Inspection arms
When you are standing still
And there are many more drills
While marching and digging in your heals

Right and Left o-bleak
Column of two's to the right or left
Mark time March, the Forward march
And of course you'll be doing it in your sleep

Now you are in your Dress Greens
Looking really sharp
Your drill Sergeant, calling out the cadence
And we all started to march

Now you can see the Grand Stand
Way in front of you
Where all the important people are
Waiting for your passing review

To see all Ninety Men marching today
And the Band playing for the final parade
With the whole Battalion digging in those heals
And if you were a Marine, it will give you chills

Our Drill Sergeant with his cadence calls
Is something you will never forget
Wishing you were still in the Corp again
Feels like, I've never really left

Cpl, Rodwick J. Padilla
USMC
Viet Nam, Veteran 66-67

Once A Marine, Always A Marine

The United States Marine Corps
What does it mean too me
Joining an elite group of Men
Who will always protect our country

For over 250 years
We are at our very best
Doing all odd jobs
Even protecting our U.S. President

There are no Mountains high
And no valleys low
And no Rivers wide enough
From keeping a Marine from doing his job

From WW I to WW2
From Guadalcanal to Korea
From Viet Nam to Iraq
Where always first in, and always the last back

I know Gods in Heaven
And has Marines guarding his gates
Who will always protect and serve
Especially if you had ran out of faith

Once a Marine, Always a Marine
Is the word of the wise
And you and you alone
Feel proud to say "Semper Fi"

"Huh Rah"

Cpl, Rodwick J. Padilla
USMC
Viet Nam, Veteran 66-67

Your Personal Gear

In Viet Nam, you're issued at least
Two pairs of clothing all year
Also issued two pairs of Combat boots
Plus, I wore my Hawaiian shorts, I sometimes feared

It makes me a bulls-eye target
Anyone can hit from 500 yards or more
It's really bright with colored flowers on it
Which is my good luck piece, I had always wore

We also had been issued a body armor flak jacket
Which I thought was really safe to wear
It's supposed to stop the bullets, and shrapnel
So go ahead, and ask all those guys who are here no more

And the most important thing is your helmet
That is much larger than your head
It's supposed to keep that little brain safe
From getting it splattered all over the place

And of course you're issued a backpack
To keep our food and dried cloths in
And also we kept our Kodak Camera, and writing paper
To keep our memories of places we have been

Then our Ammo belt, that's around your waist
Where we keep our bullets and grenades on
And our water canteens, and our bayonet
And a 45-caliber pistol, which was really hard to get

And our main part of our gear
is our weapon, that was our M-16
It's really light and small
But it will do the right thing

We always keep our personal gear intact
And packed up only what's needed
Because, once you have been on a mission
You'll know next time, it should be an easy decision

Cpl: Rodwick J. Padilla
USMC
Viet Nam, Veteran 66-67

The Day I Almost Died

It was a hot and sunny day
While resting in Camp
Taking a little smoke break
While lying in my tent

It was my off day today
I didn't have anything to do
So, I decided to go to the latrine
That's what we call restroom in the Marines

To get there is not too difficult
You can even see it from my door
Because of the rain and the mud
The trail was not a trail no more

Today I decided to walk barefooted
Like I've done many times before
Because I am from Hawaii
I did not know what was in stored

My buddy and I got to the latrine safely
And we did our little thing
While we were making our way back
Boy, I gave a violent scream

I'm feeling a very sharp pain
Like someone had stabbed my foot
And when I looked down to see what happened
I thought my goose was cooked

Their I notice tiny puncher holes
Which blood was seeping from
That means that something had bite me
And boy it hurts like a son of a gun

Not thinking at first I had
Jumped up and started screamed with joy
When I saw that green and yellow snake
Then I said "Oh Boy"

I knew I was in lots of trouble
If I didn't acted right away
I pulled out my K-Bar knife
And told my friend Goodie to slice away

Goodie said to me that he would suck out the poison
And I said it was ok with me
I had asked Goodie if he had any infection in his mouth
Because if he did, he probably die before me

I was put in too a chopper
Which it had taken me across the bay
To a very far away Hospital
Hoping that they would save my life today

I woke up on the operating table
Hearing voices saying to me
What kind of rat had bite you
I said Bamboo Viper fool

I woke hours later
With one leg up in the air
I was still in lots of pain
Which they have given me lot of Novocain

I was in bed for at least a month
Wanting to get back with the grunts
I really wanted to get out of this place
So someone else can use this space

I made a promise to. kill me a viper
And a male, or female it didn't matter
And if I did, I would let it be known
That I got one, and now I can go home

One day while I was on an operation
I decided to do a little investigation
I stuck my hand behind a very large vase
Hoping to find something with in that space

In a split second I pulled out my hand
Thought of a snake that could bite me again
I decided to move the vase a few feet away
And their it was, it had made my day

It was green and yellow in color
My friend had started screaming and hollering
It made me feel very, very lucky
To get my Bamboo Viper Trophy

I had cut its head off with my knife
Put it close to my face to see it fight
And I had spat at it because I was happy
And it almost bit my nose; I would have felt really crappie

Then I took its wiggling body
And rapped it around my neck
And a made a nut so it would stay there
To let everyone know that their was nothing to fear

There is an old saying about a snake bite in Nam
If you get bit on your behind
Guess what, you are probably going to die
Because, there is no one who is going to kiss your ass where
    the sun don't shine

Cpl: Rodwick J. Padilla
USMC
Viet Nam, Veteran 66-67

Why Did I Start Smoking

I never had smoked before
And never knew why I had started
I did know it was bad for me
And it made my parents broken hearted

I started to smoke in Boot Camp
When it was called "The Smoking Lamp Is Lit"
I thought if I stood in line and smoked
I wouldn't have to clean up, and do shit

I only started with two cigarettes at first
Which I thought it wasn't that bad
After I graduated from Boot Camp
Now I'm smoking a pack and a half

While in the country of Viet Nam
had started smoking much more
I was really trying not to make it a habit
Yet if got out of hand for sure

I remember buying my first Zippo lighter
It was a really neat thing to have
Did a lot of fancy tricks with it
Because I had to much free time off hand

Every time someone pulls out a cigarette
You automatically pull out your lighter
You try to be quick on the draw
And hope they will offer you a cigarette later

I remember the first night at the movies
I had ran out of smokes
I had asked everyone around me
Because that was the day, I was broke

Then someone passed me a rolled up smoke
Which I've never seen one before
I took a couple of hits off it
And passed it over my shoulder

Then it made its way back to me
And I had taken a couple more hits
Then I passed it back to the owner
And thanked him for that little bit

When a couple of minutes later
I started laughing out loud
The movie was not very funny
Yet their was laughter all about

I could never stop laughing
And people told me to quiet down
I didn't snap to what they were saying
Until the Sergeant had come around

I was told I had to leave the movie
So I decided to head back to my tent
Couple of my friends had followed me
Because they know I had lost my sense

Of directions I meant
Because of the darkness and gully's
My friends thought I was having too much fun
They thought I would have gotten lost, and shoot off my guns

I was still not thinking straight
Of what was really happening
I had decided to take a late shower
Even though it was in the late hours

The showers is located
Right in back of the mess hall
On the slope side of a hill
That's what I do recall

All of a sudden
The night skies had lighted up
As if it was daylight
So thought everyone in sight

I had panic for a moment
Because of the screaming, I got some chills
When I had started to leave the shower
I had slipped and fell all the way to the bottom of the hill

Because of the rain
The hillside got really slippery
And as stoned as I was
It didn't make it any easier for me

I was trying to get to my weapon
Which I had a hard time doing
I was glad no one had been watching me
Because I felt like I was a fool

Now, the lights had disappeared
And the noise had also cleared
And I'm all naked and covered with mud
And getting stared at from my buddies above

I had found out later
That it was our B-52s
Dropping their bombs
And it had scared the VC's too

I will never forget that night
As long as I live
I had smoked that rolled up cigarette
Which a real friend wouldn't have gave

Cpl: Rodwick J. Padilla
USMC
Viet Nam, Veteran 66-67

That Little Village

That Little Village
Right outside our Main Gate
Gives us a little time to relax
And maybe a little time to escape

From sitting around
Cleaning all our weapons
Or smoking cigarettes
Hoping for things to happen

There's not too much
To do in that little village
But to get a haircut, or a very close shave
Or buy souvenirs, which those people had made

While walking through the village
You can see the people's faces
If the kids are playing and having fun
You would think that the people are safe

But when the elders are not happy
It means something is not right
They will give us a hint or two
That a VC, is near in sight

They will give us a nod to who he or she is
And we will take that person in
Most of the time the villagers are right
And a VC will be put in prison

I remember one dreadful morning
It happened right outside our Main Gate
When a beautiful little girl we all knew
Had a saddened look on her face

When.my. buddy went to her aid
To see what was wrong
When she decided to kill herself
And had taken my buddy along

That little girl who had done this
Really had no choice
She killed herself to save her family
You'd think the VC's have any remorse

Times like this, it makes us think
How cruel people can be
And to put little children's life
As if there not even worth a penny

For that Marine who had died
He did not know what had hit him
He's on his way to the Pearly Gates
To protect and serve our own true faith (Semper Fi—Do Or
    Die)

Cpl: Rodwick J. Padilla
USMC
Viet Nam, Veteran 66-67

The Lonely Road

One day on my own
I had walked down this lonely road
To visit a friend of mind
I was not sure where to go

I had walked at least two miles
Before someone had stop
And asked me, if I need a lift
Of course I said why not

He was not an American
But he was driving an American Jeep
He was hiding something from me
And I found out, it was lots of fresh meat

It was nice of him to stop
Hoping it wouldn't be a surprise
Felt as if he needed me
To get through the next check point alive

Seeing from a far distance away
That the guard gate was not being raised
Now I know something must be wrong
For the soldiers had been standing in its way

Both soldiers had walked around our jeep
To see what they could find
Than one started talking to the driver
While the other kept watching me from behind

One had lifted up the canvas
To see what was hidden
And found a bunch of meat
Now they had made a decision

They both started grabbing at the meat
Without even asking
It made me very angry
I wanted to shoot them while laughing

They both looked at me
When they heard my bolt housing being pulled back
They saw that crazy look on my face
Then they both step aside, and told us to go on bye

Now a few miles down the road
I made him pull the jeep over
Took out all his meat
And put it on the shoulder

I told him I was taking his jeep
That there was nothing he could do
He never said a word
And I said have a good morning to you

While driving down the road
I saw a city bus
It turned into the tree line
Which I had stopped not far behind

Waited for a few minutes
To see who was existing the bus
Notice a friend of mine
Which I haven't seen for a long time

Like a fool, I got really close to her
Without even thinking
Putting those peoples lives in jeopardy
Guess what she had said to me

Fi-Apple, look slowly to your left
I saw this human head stuck on a pole
It was the village chief, I had been told
So I had decided I had better go

Out of the village I drove
Down that lonely highway
I had ditch the jeep into the bush
And had made it back to my troops

The very next day I had mention to my buddies
What I had done was not very funny
They said I could have been killed
That no one would have known, not even my "Gunny"

My buddies had asked me why I did it
I said I don't even know why
And they asked me if I would do it again
I said yes, but next time I'll bring a friend

Cpl: Rodwick J. Padilla
USMC
Viet Nam, Veteran 66-67

Hiking through the Paddies

Early one morning
Before leaving our ship
Where're packed up and ready
For another glories trip

Leaving our flight deck
In our HK-34 Choppers
Heading for the huge green land
And it's about 50 kilometers

Looking down from the sky
The killing fields you can see
Really long but not as wide
With dikes about two foot high

As peaceful looking down, from up there
And looking around for the green or red flares
Too let us know if the enemy is nearby
Wondering, if you will live or die

To go a hundred yards
It should take at least a few minutes
But when the shit hits the fan
You wish you weren't in it

And while the bullets are flying
You can hear people crying
And you are up to your neck in mud
Saying a silent prayer to the man above

I was shock to here this funny sound
A "bugle" blowing in the background
Going, tot, tot, tot, tot, was its call
Watching the NVA charge, and charge they all

Now I thought I saw it all
Like Indians and Cowboys, I could recall
Being pinned down by all the gun fire
And we hadn't got the support that was acquired

Then, Corporal Sanders had jumped out of his ditch
And started shooting his M-60 from his hip
Everyone was yelling for Sanders, to get on down
Until we saw him, fall lifeless to the ground

We knew what he had done, was not very smart
Thought he was John Wayne, acting his part
So we all did what Sander's had done
Didn't make it right, but the NVA started to run

It wasn't much longer
Before the shooting had stopped
Counting all the dead bodies
That we all had rounded up

We lost only a hand full of men
And it could have been worst
For every "Marine" that died
We will kill ten of them, and that's our verse

Cpl: Rodwick J. Padilla
USMC
Viet Nam, Veteran 66-67

Body Carrier

To be a Body Carrier
Sounds really weird
But you're told its part of your job
And theirs nothing to fear

I can still picture my first time
I had to carry many dead bodies up the stairs
From the hanger deck, to the second floor
To the shower rooms, we had left outside its doors

When I had walked into the room
And notice a lot of my dead friends
Lying on that wet and cold floors
Wondering, "are they really dead for sure"

After the bodies are finished being cleaned
And put into those green zipped up bags
We're to take them to the Refers below
Where the frozen food are kept

I will never forget this one corpse
That had slipped out of my hands
When it fall out of the metal basket
Down the metal stairs, again, again, and again

I had ran down after it
To the very bottom of the stairs
Saying words in this manner
That I was sorry, I hope you're not badly hurt

When my friends made me realized
That I was talking to a dead person
All my friends are staring at me
Telling me I probably need a long vacation

I had notice their was no refer doors
But a port hole instead
I decided to enter it feet first
When I had almost shit my pants

That someone or something
Had grabbed the back of my legs-
Boy, I got out of that hole so fast
I had laid rubber over that dead Marine's chest

I got a few steps up the stairs
Then I had turned around, too take a peak
To see what had grabbed me, wondering
Was it a ghost? "Hell no" it was my buddy Pete

He had been hiding in the Refer
Eating away at the fruits
He heard, we were coming down
So he decided to act like a clown

At first I wanted to kill him
But I realized, we were all in the same boat
Now I'm talking to all those dead bodies
Saying to them, hoping they have a safe trip home

Cpl: Rodwick J. Padilla
USMC
Viet Nam Veteran 66-67

The Little Plastic Toy

Spending time in Country
For the first six month
There were talks of a very new weapon
And of course it was for the grunts

So we left the Country of Viet Nam
To go to the Marine Base on Okinawa
To get our brand new assault weapon
Which it has never been in any combat action

I have received that weapon
And I was really surprised
Too see this little plastic toy
Wondering, "If we will ever survive"

We are putting it through a lot of testing
For a week at the rifle range
To make sure it works alright
Because you and it will be engaged

Now for the next seven months
My Baby and I will be as one
I'll always make sure she's clean
And oiled, and of course ready for fun

Where on our way back to Nam
To try out this new weapon
On another Search & Destroy
To put this Baby in action

Today, I'm on a five man patrol
Making sure the area is cleared
Didn't expect to find anything
When some V.C. had appeared

When I had yelled out loud, "La Dai"
It-meant-for-them-to-come over here
But they all started to run
And they had almost disappeared

I had opened fire with my baby
When something had gone wrong
My first round that I had shot
Which was a tracer, went bouncing off the ground

I told my men to open fire
But they just stared at me
So I had grabbed one of their weapons
And started firing into the trees

I knew I had hit one of them
Because I had seen him fall
And when I got to where he was
The body was not there at all

Yes, the body was gone
Where he had supposed to have fallen
His buddies had taken him away
Now my temperature is boiling

While making our way back to camp
I saw a house between the trees
I had decided to check it out
Trying to find those VC's

I had notice that little old man
Whom I saw running from us earlier
Holding an ID card in front of his face
Telling us there's no VC's on his place

So I asked him
Why had he run from us
He said, he thought that we were VC's
I said yea, right 2 Blacks, I Mexican, I White, and me

As I was looking around
I had notice a underground tunnel
That was right in back of me
And hidden in between the trees

I decided to take Ma-Ma son
With me into the tunnel
Which she had agreed
Telling us that there's no VC.

I mentioned to the old man, and my men
That if I hear any shooting going on
That Ma-Ma son will be shot in the head
And my men probably thought I was joking

So now I'm in the tunnel
With a 45 pointed to the. back of her head
Hoping nothing would happen
Which now I'm getting a little afraid

I'm ten feet into the tunnel now
When I had heard a popping noise
In a split second I saw that muzzle flash
And I didn't know if I had made the right choice

"Shit" I had killed someone
And it was for nothing
Because of those Blacks who had shot into the air
And Pa-Pa son screaming in despair

I had told the Serge
I am going to kill those Blacks
He told me to forget about it
And for us to make our way back

We did all this for General Hockmuth
Because we knew he was coming on down
Now that the perimeter had been cleared
We're watching his Chopper touch ground

The General wanted answers
Of what was happening out there
I said, PFC. Padilla reported as ordered, "Sir"
And told him what he really wanted to hear

I said Sir, that everything was fine
And that no one was hurt
That we got into a little mishap
And which the enemy had dispersed

I didn't want to mention
What really had happened out their
Serge telling me not to say anything
Because the General wouldn't care

I took a step back
As I was being dismissed
The General said good work Lance Corporal
While the Lieutenant was listening to all this

We had mentioned about our weapon getting jammed
And that no one knew really why
We were told to turn in our AR-15
And to get a new weapon called M-16

Years later I had found out what had happened
I had been watching TV, and it talked about the AR-15
And what had caused our weapon to jam under fire
That lots of Marines had died, because of some ones desire

That the powder was the wrong kind of powder
And that the bolt housing was not chromed
And our U.S. Government knew about this
They all just watched "as our Dead Marines went home"

Cpl: Rodwick J. Padilla
USMC
Viet Nam, Veteran 66-67

Marine blues: 1965—Before graduating Boot Camp at MCRD, San Diego

1966—Taken in in Da Nang, South Vietnam

Booby Traps

Something unexpected could happen
At any time of the day
Booby traps are made to kill people
They hope it would get me today

There are many types of booby traps
That the enemy had made for you
Pungi pits, were made of many pointed bamboo's
Or even bombs that had been dropped by our B-52's

Usually you can tell
When traps had been set
Especially on the main roads
And that's as close as they would get

We do mine sweeps
Once in a while
With a metal detector
We will go at least a couple of miles

We find 500 and 1000 lb bombs
That's been buried at least a few feet under
So when the tanks or trucks drive over it
You will hear a large thunder

When you see those vehicles
That has been blown up
Surprise if anyone could survive
The large explosions from the underside

I had found my first booby trap
That no one had ever seen before
It was made of bamboo, and a 45 round
And it was buried a few inches in the ground

Instead of me stepping on it
I had accidentally trip on it by luck
When I had pulled it out of the ground
There it was, a single 45 round

I had put all three pieces together
The bullet and the two pieces of bamboo
And if the 45 round would of gone off
It would not only blown off my shoe

Also snakes had been found
In the underground tunnels
They are very hard to see
And their bites are also very deadly

They say, when walking down the trails
Do not jump into the side ditches
Because of the old rusted metal stakes
Raped with human shit all over it

Pungi pit baskets, comes in all sizes
From shallow or deep, or wide or narrow
But there is one thing for sure
If you step in it, you will give a violent roar

I had seen one of my friends
Step onto one about knee high
When he started screaming for help
A couple of seconds later he was shot between the eyes

Till this day in Viet Nam
People are still getting hurt or killed
Too bad there is no easy way
To clear out the huge killing fields

Cpl: Rodwick J. Padilla
USMC
Viet Nam Veteran 66-67

Just Another Operation

The night before a major operation
We are gathering up all our provisions
Taking only what is needed
Too help us survive the scorching heat

It's only 2 A.M. in the early morning
And now my blood pressure is really boiling
We were saying goodbye to our fellow friends
Which we may not ever see them again

Lights throughout the ship are white no more
Just before we all have to go ashore
Red lights give us the sense of death
And that feeling you' 11 never forget

I've been through this a many times before
Makes you never forget what's really in store
You'll always think of bad things that would happen
That will always put you in a sense of depression

I could feel my heart beating really fast
Reminding us that it's almost time at last
When we have to disembark
Into that huge green land of killing sharks

Now that the sun is over the horizon
Trying to finish a letter to my cousin
Writing a short few words of our new operation
Hoping we won't enter a bad situation

Now my squad leader is calling out numbers
Telling us to climb into those beat up choppers
Then all together we lift off the flight deck
Towards the land of those little grass shacks

Seeing for the first time as your looking down
You see many ships lurking around
Watching the "New Jersey" shoot its big guns
While far away the "B-52s" are dropping their bombs

Then out of know where we were surprised
The enemy strong holes were disguised
Machine guns bullets were hitting us from both sides
We notice a couple of our choppers falling out of the sky

We had to change the drop off to a new location
And all the other choppers had followed in rotation
We had surprised the enemy from behind
As we moved along everything came out fine

Now that the battle had lasted over a week
Our men dropping like flies because of the heat
Then we got notice to get the hell out
This made no sense what it was all about

Yes, we were in North Viet Nam
A place we weren't supposed to have been in
We had lost many of our men
And hearing we might do it again

Now, who's telling our Dead?
It was a really big mistake
That someone had given the orders
While our Commanders played patty cake

When we were returning back to our ship
There was this huge size banner
Flying high above the main house area
Saying words in this manner

"Welcome Back 1st Battalion 3rd Marines 3rd Marine Division
For pulling the most ever Search and Destroy Missions Since
  "World War I"
It made us feel a little good at first
But the lives we had lost was like a curse

We made it back from another big fight
Resting up for the next one near in sight
How many more men must we lose?
To win a un-winnable war, we did not chose

Now that we had lost thousands of men
Is there anything we could say to them?
What the hell we were fighting for
Especially when this wasn't considered a war

A conflict it was called
Or a police action on the other hand
You realized these people didn't even care
They most likely wanted us out of there

So I'm here writing this story
Hoping you would feel a little sorry
For those who died, will feel no pain
For our Country who had nothing to gain

In the future "War" will go on
Men will die, and people will shun
Your "Kids" kids could be next
If they don't fall through the political cracks

Cpl: Rodwick J. Padilla
USMC
Viet Nam, Veteran 66-67

Time for R&R

When you have been in Country
For at least six months or more
You're allowed to take a vacation
This is called Rest and Recreation

You can go to Australia, or Hong Kong
Tokyo, Manila, even Banqlok
Kuala Lumpur, or Singapore
You'll have lots of fun for sure

And if you don't want to go anywhere
You can stay back in Country
Too one of the nicest beach anywhere in the world
It's called China Beach, and I have been there

Then, for the married men
They want to see their wives
They are allowed to go to Hawaii
And the Military will pay for their flights

The next vacation you'll get
Is when you finish your 13 month tour
Leaving Viet Nam, on a Pan Am 747
Thanking God, for who is their in Heaven

Cpl: Rodwick J. Padilla
USMC
Viet Nam, Veteran 66-67

Sea Rations

It comes in a box
About 6 inch by 6 inch
It's called Sea Rations
Actually, it was like a little present

It comes with a can of fruit
Different kinds of course
Once in a while a can fruit cake
Or a can of fruit cock tail of that sort

The main dish everyone knew I liked
Was a can of pork with beans
My buddies really didn't like me eating that
Because they knew I would do the stinky thing

There was also a pack of cookies
And a small pack of cigarettes
Either kools or marlboros was the brands
And if you didn't smoke, you gave it to a friend

Also a pack with a small blue pill
That we all didn't really like
It's used to heat up our food
But you'll be in tears for a while

So most of time
We ate our food cold
Because where always on the run
Or Vietnamese food, yum, yum, yum

To open the cans of fruit and food
We used a military can opener
It's really small and light
We keep it around our neck, and taped really tight

I remember that one night
We were packing our backpacks
And a friend of mind had asked me
Should he take the can food he never liked

I had told him it might save his life one day.
So he decided to throw it into his pack
Now where're landing in the LZ
He had jumped out of the chopper in front of me

I heard shots fired
And my buddy had fallen towards me
I knew that he had gotten shot
And you would not believe what you would see

I had pulled off his backpack
To see where he had been shot
There was a bullet stuck in his flap jacket
Which he got a huge black and blue spot

I had opened up his backpack
To see what had help stop the bullet
It was that can food he never liked
But yet, he knew it had saved his life

He gave me this look
As if he didn't believe what had happened
He said he was glad, that he did what I've said
And if he didn't, he would have been dead

Cpl. Rodwick J. Padilla
USMC
Viet Nam, Veteran 66-67

Statue of Liberty

The Statue of Liberty
It's a game you only play at night
Not just anyone would like to play it
And yet I know, I did play it twice

I wonder what had made me play that game
I don't really know
Thought it was fun at the time
And this is the way it goes

You will jump out of your fox hole
And hold up your right hand in the air
Striking your Zippo lighter
Making that little fire appear

You can see the flame
From at least a mile away
Wishing the enemy will open fire
Then it will be your tum, to make your bullets go a-stray

Hoping to hit your target
Maybe two or three
By then the enemy will disappear
Because of the daylight that has appeared

The enemy likes to hit and run
Because they know that area really well
So by playing the' game of Statue of Liberty
It could keep you and your men from getting killed

Cpl: Rodwick J. Padilla
USMC
Viet Nam, Veteran 66-67

Between the Cracks

Spending 395 days in country
Would make anyone feel a little jumpy
Either you're hiking in the mountains
Or walking in the rice paddies

As we staggered through the mud
Nearly side by side
Trying not to scare the birds
Letting the VCs know, that we're nearby

I had always wondered why
When our unit enters into the open
That it makes us all very easy targets
And yet there are other safe locations

Waiting for the one special moment
When the unexpected would happen
We would all fall to the ground
Because of the incoming rounds

Now it early midday
And the temperature is rising
And there is no shade to hide
Except only your helmet will provide

We were all getting this very bad feeling
That something was going to go wrong
And there was nothing anyone could have done
As we all kept moving right along

All of a sudden
We started hearing gun fire
Echoing sounds are coming from behind
And where all in the open and nowhere to hide

The faster you get out of the open
Into the tree lines up ahead
You'll try to stay very calm
And of course you will be using your head

Now my buddy Ski, had hit the ground
I said to him to get on up
He said to me, no way
Not until the shooting stops

It did stop a few seconds later
When I heard Ski, gave a funny sound
Like a very deep grunt
While his face had been buried into the ground

I had a feeling that Ski had been shot
If you guest where, you would be right
Yea, where the sun don't shine
Yes, right up his be-hind

Now Ski, is in a lot of pain
I had called for a medic, to take him away
They threw him into a Chopper
And I never saw him again, after that day

Ski will be home soon
Partying with his friends
Because of his million dollar wound
He will be a Civilian again

We had all promised to meet one day
After we all returned back home
And have a beer or two
But that day, had never come

I never did get a chance
To see my buddy Ski
Because I got into a little trouble
And I ended up in the Penitentiary

Cpl: Rodwick J. Padilla
USMC
Viet Nam Veteran 66-67

Elephant Grass

Walking through the tall elephant grass
There's not much you can see
Hope you don't run into any booby traps
Waiting around the comer for me

I remember my very first time
On an early sunny morning
Walking through that thick elephant grass
We usually don't get much warning

There were men in front of me
Who had been screaming and hollering
Saying, there are a lot of VC's
To take cover, so we got down on our knees

Luckily we did that
Cause the VC's were shooting chest high
And if we would have been standing
Most of us would have died

I had been carrying 81 motor rounds
At least 3 of them on my back
When I decided to fall to the ground
I was praying, I won't get hit by those in coming rounds

I had outstretched both of my hands
After laying on the ground
Had put both hands over the top of my helmet
So the bullets wouldn't hit my 81 motor rounds

Boy, did I panic for a few seconds
Didn't know what to expect
I had rolled fully around now
Still trying to protect those 81 motor rounds

I started ripping off my back pack
And was free to move around
Just about to get on up off the ground
When my serge told me to stay down

I wanted to shoot back
At what I really couldn't see
I just had to wait they said
Until the really got close to me

Then someone yelled out, I can see them
When the shooting got much louder
I got up and ran forward like a crazy man
Shooting, screaming, and hollering

I had panic before
But not like this
If you were in the Elephant Grass
You'll probably do the same shit

It had only lasted a few minutes
And the enemy had disappeared
The VC's like to hit and run
They have been doing that since the war begun

Cpl: Rodwick J. Padilla
USMC
Viet Nam, Veteran 66-67

My Silver Star Moment

It was real early in the morning
About six miles from land
We were all packed up and ready
To do another Search and Destroy again

All the Choppers that are on the flight deck
Are all warming there engines
And about ready to take us all
To an unknown destination

We are up in the clouds really high
Hope we don't get shot out of the sky
Circling around for a few minutes
While coming down we could hear the bullets

Do-Do-Do-Do-Do was its sound
It was the VC's firing, 50 caliber rounds
We all took cover in ditches, located in the middle of the field
It was the only place to hide, surprise no one had gotten killed

It seem like only a few minutes
When my serge had called out for me
I was told to report to him in a hurry
Then he told me, we got lots to worry

He said the men were dropping like flies
Because of no shade, and the temp being 105
And that we were out of water, and I gave him both of mine
Serge said we need water soon, or most of them will die

I told the Serge of a water hole I've seen earlier
It was a few clicks behind, next to those tall green trees
I was told to go ahead and do the best I could
So I made a plan that I thought it was good

I had decided to do it myself
Put a bunch of canteens and strapped it to my belt.
Also I had taken off my boots, though I would run much faster
Yea, me and my skinny ass, hope it won't be a disaster

Before I had jumped out of the hole
I had asked my buddies for some protection
All they had to do was shot towards the hill
Ever precious seconds would help me from getting killed

Now I'm out, and running about
Trying to make it to the trees up ahead
Bullets were popping all around me
And if I don't run any faster I will be dead

Then I had said to myself, zigzag fool
This made a lot of sense at that time
With me running in a straight line
It made me an easy target from behind

Now I had entered the tree line
And started looking for the water hole
I had went in about 20 yards deep
And found water just below my feet

I started filling the canteens with dirty water
Notice mosquitoes, had been swimming all about
I supposed to have put malaria pills in each canteen
Knowing my recollection, I couldn't remember anything

Also I had notice a little too late
I didn't bring any kind of weapon with me
To protect myself from the enemy
Just hope I run fast, and make it back free

Started to make my way back
To the edge of the tree line
Standing in the shadows, I could see my men
Who had been pinned down for very long time

I signaled to my men, I'm coming in
For them to open fire, to give me protection again
Started running my butt off, with those heavy canteens
Now both foots are sinking in the sand, if you know what I
    mean

I started zigzagging on my way in
When bullets were flying around me again
When 2 jet planes started shooting their rockets
It gave a chance of not being an easy target

I dove into the hole
With all those canteens
Gave it to the men
Who were really glad, to see me again

I had no knowledge at that time
That someone wrote me up for an accommodation
I had found out two years later
While in prison, signing my discharge papers

Gunny Sergeant Colburn had mention to me
While Capt. Rusley was standing next to him
That my name had been removed
From the "Silver Star book"

I felt, "If you had earned a medal like that"
Why does it take so long for you to receive it?
Maybe if I had been killed
"I would have gotten it much faster"

Cpl: Rodwick J. Padilla
USMC
Viet Nam, Veteran 66-67

Wondering If 1 Had Ever Slept

Young as I was
And full of energy
Sleep is a wonderful word
But it was not for me

Remembering the good times
We all set around and talked
Even played a hand of poker or two
Until the light went out

Trying to get lots of rest
But your mind, saying otherwise
Gathering all your equipment that's needed
Making sure your weapons are working right

Tonight we are on night patrol
All spread out walking really slow
Ankle deep in the rice paddies
Is like walking in foot and a half of snow

I would never forget
This one special night
That there was no moon
Anywhere in sight

Because of it being really dark
Your eyes will start playing tricks
You think you see the enemy
And you don't want to even blink

Now you start hearing voices
You can't tell where it's coming from
You want to shoot your weapon
But we were told to hold on

Now my eyes are getting a little heavy
And I thought I was still awake
When someone had kicked me in the head
Which had woke me up, with a very bad headache

I had noticed my sergeant
Standing directly in back of me
Now, I just realized what had happened
When my sergeant said, He could have been a VC

I was mad at first
But I knew he was right
I could have been killed
And also everyone in sight

This was the first time
That something like this had happened to me
I had made a promise to myself
That they will not kill this "Statue of Liberty"

Cpl: Rodwick J. Padilla
USMC,
Viet Nam, Veteran 66-67

Rocket Time

Sitting around the camp fire
Telling stores of back home
When I made a whistle sound
Pretending a rocket was coming down

My friends looked at me
They thought they had heard something
I said it was me making that whistle sound
When a real rocket had touch ground

I had turned my head to the left
Where the explosion had come from
I got a glimpse of a large fire ball
It was red and yellow, and very tall

When I looked back towards my friends
Their was no one there but me
I ran and yelled "hey Goodie" where are you
When more rockets came in sprees

I heard Goodies voice
Screaming out loud for me
I'm over here in the hole
So get on in "Pineapple"

So I dove into the ditch head first
And I had said to "Goodie"
Stay where you're at
Because I had buried my head under his chests

At least a few more rockets came in
And we found out that on one got hurt
Maybe because we had prayed to the man above
While someone had shit there pants, that's what I heard

A few weeks later, it happened again
When I had been walking down the road
And I said to myself, it's been really quiet
Then I made this mistake, and whistled like a rocket

It did come down, all over the place
It didn't matter to me, which I just kept on pace
Walking down that road, to my tent up a head
While Marines are yelling at me, to get down or you'll be dead

I felt as if I could not be killed
Because, I knew I had a death wish
Like I knew that the Enemies are really bad shooters
I could stand in front of a VC firing squad, and they would all
    miss, me

Cpl: Rodwick Padilla
USMC
Viet Nam, Veteran 66-67

No Fear

It's getting towards the end
Of my 13 month tour
I felt like I had no fear
Of living, or dying, it does sound weird

I have been through a lot
And escaped death many times
Did a lot of stupid stuff
Most people would call it a crime

But when you have much hate
In your heart for losing your older brother
I felt as if there is nothing that could really stop me
From doing the right or wrong thing it didn't matter

Like walking down the road
When some rockets came flying in
People yelling at me to get on down
But I kept walking and swearing out loud

Another time I ran out of the foxhole
And getting shot at while doing so
I did it for the men who would have died
Because we needed water, and the temp was at 105

So fear is fear in itself
Which many people do feared
And if you can't conquer it now
In time, hope you'll get out of it some how

Cpl: Rodwick J. Padilla
USMC
Viet Nam, Veteran 66-67

Coming Home

You're 18 now, and all alone
You're out of school, and don't know what to do
So I've decided to join the Marines to get away
To a faraway Country for some 13 month stay

You have made a lot of friends
That you know you can depend on
While sitting around the camp fire
Telling stories of where you're from

Writing letters home to someone special
Hoping they understand what you've been through
Also while leaving out gory details
Smoking cigarettes, and drinking ginger ale

Thinking of things I've missed at home
Of how we used to talk, hours on the phone
How we used to snuggle, and how we kissed
And doing the wild thing, I really had missed

Now my days are coming to an end
Can't wait to have you in my arms once again
Now our plane has just arrived in San Diego
Hear people crying out loud, which they had given us this label

Get out of here you baby killer's
Our Country don't want you anymore
And spat at us, as we walked on bye
As we held our heads up "slightly high"

We were all very angry at first
We could have lash back
But we understood where they were coming from
So we just let it go, and gave it a lot of slack

It will take a while for people to understand
What each soldier had put their lives through
And only if we could get our lives back
From being known as "Killing Machine"

Cpl: Rodwick J. Padilla
USMC
Viet Nam Veteran 66-67

Later Years

Now I'm back home
In our god forsaking country
Hoping everything will tum out fine
Of thoughts of what was left behind

Not hearing the sounds of bombs
Exploding from far away
Or sounds of bullets
Being shot at us every day

Or finding booby traps
Figuratively, using the kitchen sink
And jumping out of our choppers
Did we know it really stinks?

Especially walking through the Elephant Grass
Much taller than any man
We knew when the shit hits the fan
You'll be crawling on your face and hands

Also going through the villages
Searching for food or weapons
It's called Search and Destroy
We're trying to leave the VC's with nothing

I've made a bad habit of smoking
I wish I've never started
But it had relaxed me a lot
I even used it of becoming a human target

Usually burning villages down
Was never a problem with me?
Because when the night comes around
The villages all belong to the VC's

Seeing "Round Eye Girls" again
It was a sour sight to see
Now I have my arms around one
I realized I'm home, and I'm feeling free

Hope your family and friends
Would remember what we all went through
To help us in every sense of the way
To bring you back to reality, "that's if you want to"

Cpl: Rodwick J. Padilla
USMC
Viet Nam, Veteran 66""67

The Viet Nam Wall

The wall is something
You all should see
Where it's located at
Is in Washington D.C

That is where all our
Brave war heroes are
Lying six foot under
Looking up at the stars

There are no Statues
Standing still
It stands eight foot tall
And it will give you chills

About 300 foot long
From end to end
This Marble figure
You've want to see again

It's memory of men
Who fought in a far away
Country For what they would have known
They had fought for nothing

Communism, they say
Will stop right here
If our Country could help
Keep South Viet Nam from fear

Men made their choices
To join or be drafted
Young or old
In all of our Military Branches

Rich or poor
Made no difference
Short or tall
Could make a preference

Many people wondered
When the war would end
It was from day to day
Until you did your span

Now, there are tens of thousands
Of names on this wall
Each has a story
And a story for all

Names are engraved
By day and year
and when they had fallen
It should appear

People had said and felt
If you close your eyes
While touching the wall
You and you alone can see them all

For me there is
A special name on this wall
Which I will never forget
And will always recall

It's my older brother
Who I had seen last
Telling we not to worry
That he'll be right back

"Yes" he did come back
In a green zip up bag
To say life is just a dream
A dream that he did not have

Now I had etched
His name off the wall
Will keep it in my folder
And to show it too you all

Please if you're in the area
Drop on by and say a few words
They love to hear from you
And of any stories you have heard

Cpl: Rodwick J. Padilla
USMC
Viet Nam, Veteran 66-67

My Life

My life as a young man
Was all but not fair
When my Mother had left us all
Without any despair

Too see her no more
We may not know when
To live a life without her
And with a new mommy, we had to pretend

Remembering the tears I had cried for years
When she wasn't there to hold us dear
And now the tears are gone forever
We may never know if it was for endeavor

We hated to dread any awful news
About my mother being abused
She wanted us to think that everything was fine
But yet we knew better from time too time

Until one day we had received a call
From a man who had told us all
He said, that she had loved us all very much
For now she's gone, and that she had missed you all very much

Now our Family wants to know
While we are getting much older
Would we ever be like our mom
To go astray, and never to be heard from

Rodwick J. Padilla, Son